Realistic
HORSES
Coloring Book

Adult Coloring Books Animals

by
Happy Arts Coloring

"Riding a horse is not a gentle hobby, to be picked up and laid down like a game of solitaire. It is a grand passion."

Ralph Waldo Emerson

WHY THIS BOOK IS DIFFERENT

This is not just another horse coloring book.

It is a journey into the world of horses - their strength, their beauty, their history, and their spirit.

Every page is hand-curated to offer more than art:
- Realistic Line Drawings - clean, bold illustrations created for adult colorists who want detail without clutter.
- Education & Inspiration - scattered trough the book you'll find fascinating horse facts, tips on care and connection, and timeless traditions from equestrian culture.
- Quotes from Literature - short, powerful passages from Black Beauty, Shakespeare, and other classic works remind us of the deep bond between horses and people.
- Mindfulness & Relaxation - each scene invites calm, creativity, and reflection, making coloring more than a pastime - it becomes a mindful escape.
- A Celebration of Horses - from Friesians in full stride to foals at play, from riders in harmony to wild herds in nature, this book honors the horse in all its forms.

Where most coloring books stop at empty outlines, this one offers a complete experience: art, knowledge, inspiration, and the timeless magic of horses.

Where most coloring books stop at empty outlines, this one offers a complete experience: art, knowledge, inspiration, and the timeless magic of horses.

This is a book made for:
- Horse lovers of all ages.
- Colorists who want a meaningful project.
- Anyone seeking calm, beauty, and connection in the simple act of coloring.

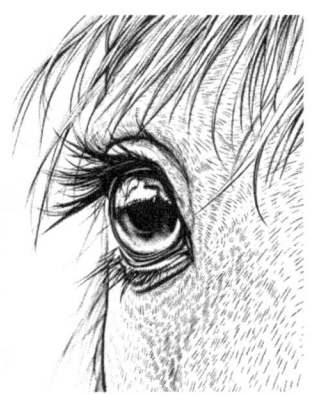

More than a coloring book.

A tribute to the horse.

FAMOUS
Horses & Stories

- Secretariat – A legendary American racehorse who won the 1973 Triple Crown, setting records still unbroken today.
- Seabiscuit – A small underdog racehorse of the 1930s who became a symbol of hope during the Great Depression.
- Alexander the Great's horse, Bucephalus – A fierce war horse said to fear only his own shadow.
- Black Beauty – The fictional horse from Anna Sewell's 1877 novel that inspired animal welfare reforms.
- Comanche – The only U.S. Cavalry horse known to survive the Battle of Little Bighorn in 1876.
- Marengo – Napoleon's famous grey Arabian warhorse, said to have carried him in many battles.
- Man o' War – One of the greatest racehorses in history, winning 20 of 21 races in the early 1900s.
- Clever Hans – A horse in early 1900s Germany believed to solve math problems, later discovered to be responding to subtle human cues.
- Trigger – The beloved golden palomino of Hollywood cowboy Roy Rogers, appearing in dozens of films.
- Traveler – The white horse of General Robert E. Lee, famous during the American Civil War.

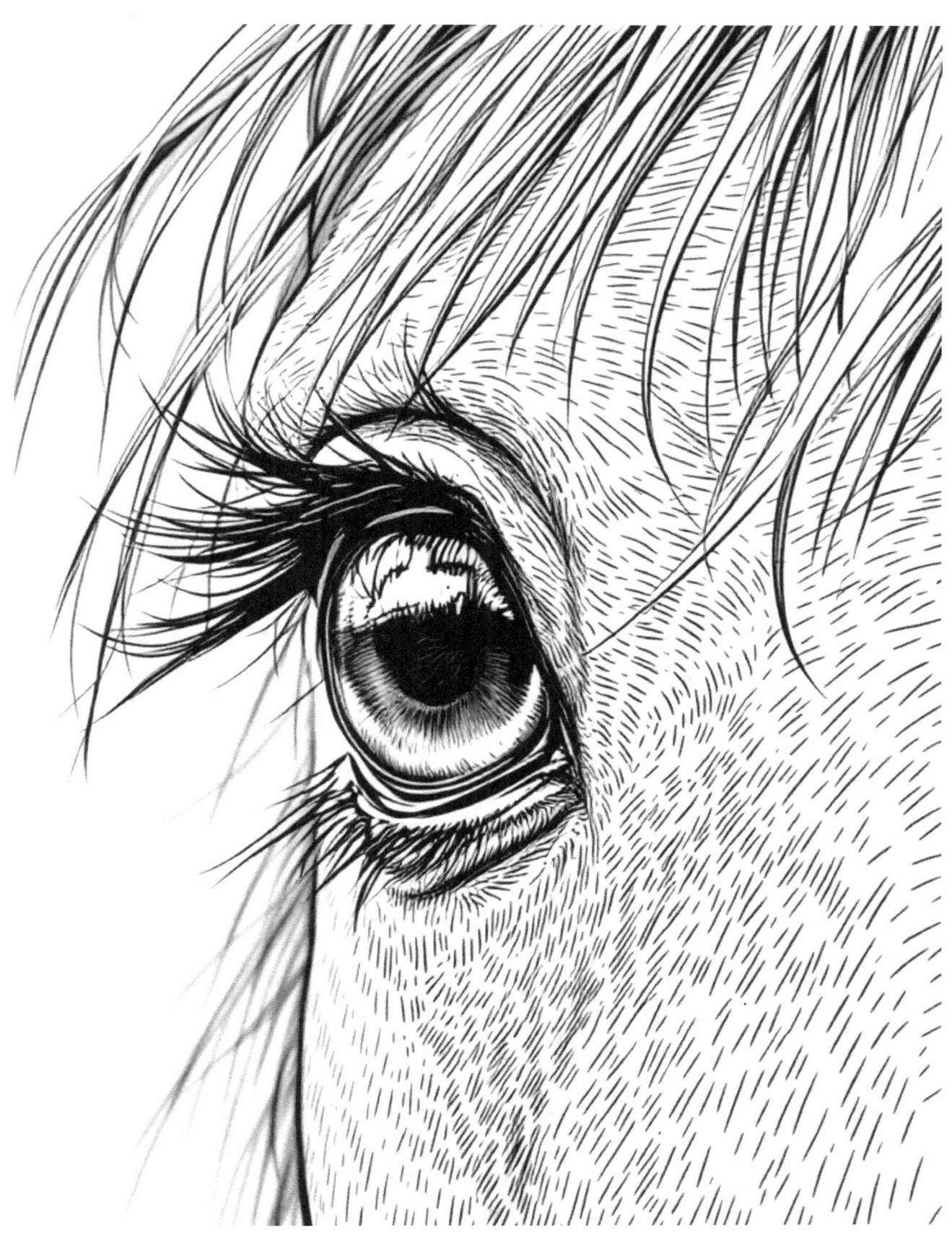

"A horse is the projection of people's dreams about themselves. strong. powerful. beautiful." Pam Brown

HORSE
Quotes from Literature

- "The horse is man's noblest companion." Aristotle (ancient texts, public domain)
- "No philosopher so thoroughly comprehends us as dogs and horses." Herman Melville (Redburn, 1849)
- "When I bestride him, I soar, I am a hawk." William Shakespeare (Henry V, Act 3, Scene 7)
- "He doth nothing but talk of his horse." William Shakespeare (Merchant of Venice, Act 1, Scene 2)
- "The horse, the horse! The symbol of surging potency and power of movement, of action in man." D.H. Lawrence (Apocalypse, 1931 — PD in US/EU).
- "Horses are taught by the spur, not the reins." Ovid (Ars Amatoria, 2 BCE).
- "Good horses make short miles." George Herbert (Jacula Prudentum, 1651).
- "The discipline of the horse is the discipline of kings." (Steinbeck Cup of Gold)
- "To ride a horse is to ride the sky." (Steinbeck poem fragment, early works collected pre-1930s — public domain)
- "Good places make good horses."Black Beauty (Anna Sewell, 1877)

"The wind of heaven is that which blows between a horses ears." Arabian Proverb

HORSE GAITS
(Walk, Trot, Canter, Gallop)

- Walk – A four-beat gait, calm and steady, about 4 miles per hour.
- Trot – A two-beat gait where diagonal legs move together, about 8 miles per hour.
- Canter – A three-beat gait, smoother and faster than a trot, around 10–17 miles per hour.
- Gallop – The fastest gait, a four-beat run, with racehorses reaching 40+ miles per hour.
- The Icelandic horse has two unique gaits: the tölt (smooth four-beat gait) and the flying pace.
- The Paso Fino breed is known for its naturally smooth, rhythmic four-beat gait.
- Wild Mustangs develop unique gait variations due to survival and terrain.
- Horses in dressage are trained to perform advanced gaits like piaffe (trot in place) and passage (elevated trot).
- A foal can usually stand and walk within one to two hours of birth.
- Some breeds, like Standardbreds, are famous for their trotting or pacing races.

"The horse. Here is nobility without conceit, friendship without envy, beauty without vanity." Ronald Duncan

FUN TRADITIONS
in Shows & Sports

- In dressage, braiding the horse's mane is a sign of respect and tradition.
- In western shows, silver-studded tack reflects pride and heritage.
- Polo ponies are often given nicknames that reflect their speed, spirit, or personality.
- At rodeos, horses are celebrated just as much as the riders - many broncs and bulls are legends themselves.
- In racing, it's considered lucky to give a horse a gentle pat on the neck before heading to the start line.
- In showjumping, many riders wear lucky charms, from special socks to braided ribbons in the horse's tail.
- Parade horses often wear colorful, decorative tack that reflects local culture and pride.
- The tradition of the victory lap, where the winner circles the arena with the flag, celebrates both horse and rider.
- In fox hunting, horses are sometimes blessed in ceremonies before the season begins, a practice known as "Blessing of the Hounds and Horses."
- Show horses are often given elaborate grooming before competition, including polished hooves and even glitter on manes for children's classes.
- Mounted games, like jousting or tent pegging, come from historic traditions where horses and riders trained for battle.

"Horses change lives. They give young people confidence and older people peace."
Toni Robinson

HORSE
Anatomy Facts

- Horses have the largest eyes of any land mammal. Each eye is about the size of a tennis ball.
- A horse's teeth take up more space in its head than its brain.
- Horses can rotate their ears almost 180 degrees - controlled by 10 different muscles.
- The average horse has 205 bones, similar to humans.
- Horses cannot breathe through their mouths - only through their nostrils.
- A horse's hoof is made of keratin, the same material as human fingernails.
- The average horse heart weighs about 10 pounds and can pump over 40 liters of blood per minute during exercise.
- Horses have an almost 360-degree field of vision, but they cannot see directly in front or behind them.
- The "frog" of a horse's hoof acts like a natural shock absorber and pump for blood circulation.
- Horses can sleep both lying down and standing up (thanks to a special "stay apparatus" in their legs).

"A man on a horse is spiritually as well as physically bigger than a man on foot." John Steinbeck

"A true horseman does not look at a horse with his eyes. he looks at his horse with his heart." Unknown

www.ingramcontent.com/pod-product-compliance
Lightning Source LLC
Chambersburg PA
CBHW080801080526
44654CB00078B/1580